The Boss's Philosophy
By P.E. Statler

©Copyright 2013

All rights reserved.

The author is not a licensed medical practitioner. Any facts views or opinions expressed in this book are not intended to cure, treat, or prevent any illness or disease. All material from other sources than the author's own mind is labeled as such. Any similarity between this work and other is purely a coincidence, and is not intentional.

The Boss's Philosophy Copyright © 2013 by P.E. Statler

All rights reserves. No part of this work may be reproduced or copied in any form by any means-including electronic, photocopying, information storage and retrieval systems-without written permission of the author.

Dedication

This book is dedicated to all my enemies.

Without you I would not have the ambition to succeed.

I thank you.

Definition of a Boss:

A boss is someone who has control of his (or her) life. He knows what is going on around him and has the mentality to react to any changes that may occur and benefit from them. Smooth, yet subtle, he influences his environment in a way that promotes success for all. Like a magnet, others find themselves attracted to his presence without knowing why. A true boss radiates success and inspiration, personally and professionally, he will prosper.

About The Author:

In 2008 P.E. Statler was wrongfully convicted and sentenced to 41 years in prison. For years highly talented attorneys fought to prove his innocence, and after 4 1/2 years they succeeded. P.E. Statler was released on December 14th 2012. He now lives in Spokane Washington.

During his incarceration P.E. Statler wrote this short yet powerful book titled "The Boss's Philosophy". Sense his release he has began to work on other books including a children's book and a memoir focusing on the events behind is wrongful conviction.

Index

Introduction..*page 8*

Chapter One

A Leader's Foundation.. *page 12*

Chapter Two

Observe the World...and be Wise in its Ways......... *page 17*

Chapter Three

The Silent Move is the Wise One..............................*page 22*

Chapter Four

People Have Bad Attitudes…Not Bad Days.............*page 26*

Chapter Five

Fearlessness is the Essence of Freedom................*page 31*

Chapter Six

Veni, Vidi, Vici..*page 35*

Chapter Seven

Develop a Network to be Reckoned with...................*page 43*

Chapter Eight
Soldiers and Soul Mates..*page 48*

Chapter Nine

Am I My Brother's Keeper?..*page 56*

Chapter Ten

Visualize Success in your Future.............................*page 61*

Chapter Eleven

The Truth, the Light, the Way...................................*page 66*

Chapter Twelve

The King's Strategy..*page 72*

Introduction

Today, just as always, people struggle in vain to attain success. The majority of one's lifetime is often spent on a fruitless journey for material gains. As a result their relationships suffer, the money they earn never seems to satisfy, and happiness has become a distant memory it not a complete myth. Most of us live day to day in a state of "tunnel vision" and the sad truth is that it often takes a major life crisis to get our attention.

The quality of life is determined by the choices you make, and if your life is not perfect there is still room for growth. By taking charge of your life you effectively become "boss" of your environment. This is the true essence of a self made leader. In reality there is no President or politician who can snap his or her fingers and bring about the changes you desire in your life. There is no $800 billion dollar stimulus package with your name on it, happiness cannot be bought, and Santa Claus is not real. But dreams do come true and ultimately it is up to you to decide if they do.

The Boss's Philosophy is written in short, clear chapters designed to keep your attention. These chapters will provide you with the keys you need to be successful in every area of your life. In addition, they will teach you how to eliminate all of your life's problems no matter what they are because although the problems in your life may change from day to day, the remedy is always the same. When you begin to apply the Boss's Philosophy you will notice the changes immediately. Days become full of new experiences, relationships will grow, money will come without the stress, anxiety turns into confidence, and worldly vices will lose their grip. Your love life will also benefit immensely. All of the things that were once out of reach will no longer be impossible as you begin to discover your true potential.

Before we continue I must explain the seriousness of what has been said up to this point.

It is an absolute certainty that if you seriously apply what you learn from this book you will find meaningful success.

In most cases the increases that you experience will far exceed your expectations. Understand that this meaningful success come from having a pure knowledge of what your place in this world is and how it affects other people. It is your God given right to experience the finer things in life and no man or government can deprive you of that. But with this knowledge comes power over others, and you must exercise it appropriately or you will fail in all that you do. Those who master this have no limits to what they can accomplish.

"Ignorance is not bliss, it is a comfortable prison cell"

We live in a time where greed, corruption, and hidden agendas cloud our personal and professional lives. Tax payers have become an abused vein for the government to leach upon without consequence. The financial institutions that we put so much trust into operate with no integrity. Politicians reign un-policed. Terrorists pervert religion in order to promote violence. Men and women everywhere trade their fear of God for fancy cars, and everyday miracles are aborted. It is no hard task to understand why most people struggle to succeed in life.

The fact that you are reading this book proves that you are ready to increase your level of success and once you have finished reading you will be equipped with the knowledge that it takes to do just that. You cannot go through life being afraid of change. Historically, it has always been the people who have constantly strived to better themselves that find lasting success. These people learned at an early age to embrace change. When you are mentally prepared for the "hard balls" that life throws your way your chance of hitting a "home run" increases tenfold.

"As a man thinks in his heart…so shall it be" Proverbs 3:27

The Boss's Philosophy is a combination of common sense, creativity and hidden knowledge. When taken together it is a fool proof recipe for success. A boss is someone who is in control of his or her life.

What I mean by this is that a boss knows what is going on around him and has the mentality to react to any changes that may occur and benefit from them. There is nothing selfish or evil about being successful, in fact, when you're on top of your game you will find that it brings you pleasure to help others. After all, a generous man is a wise man. It is important to remember that success is not defined by the amount of money in your bank account. I know many unhappy people with lots of money. I know broke people full of joy. But the keys in this book will teach you how to generate wealth and balance your finances and relationships in a way that promotes happiness. All you must do is apply what you learn.

I wrote this with the intention of inspiring you to become something greater than you are now. If this book provides you with that much needed spark then my mission is accomplished. Don't spend your life waiting for a second chance to succeed, this is it. This is your call to greatness. I believe each of us has the ability to live a life of purpose and success, and when you never give up nothing can stand between you and your dreams.

"Once you learn to lead yourself...others will follow"

Yours Truly,
P.E. Statler

A Leaders Foundation

Chapter One

Before you can advance your level of success in any area of your life you must first have an honest understanding of who you really are. You will have to identify all of your strengths and weaknesses so you will know where to improve. The things that define you are personality, character and people skills. Even the smallest flaws in any of these areas can prevent you from reaching your goals. For example, if I had an anger problem it could be preventing me from communicating openly with people. As a result, business and relationships could suffer in a major way. As a boss you must be completely in sync with yourself before you can expect to find success among others. Each of us has flaws and areas that we need to improve in, so don't get discouraged when you begin to identify yours. Take a moment and think about the things you would like to change about yourself, and be honest. You have nothing to lose.

After you have identified the areas that need some improvement, you can begin to grow in those areas. In most cases, you will be able to eliminate those flaws simply by focusing on them throughout the day and making the conscious decision to remove them from your life. When you're conscious of the things you need to change about yourself, you can stop them before they happen. I call this "self corrective behavior." After a day or two you will spend less and less time thinking about correcting your problems because it will have become second nature for your brain to perform the task on its own. Essentially, you will have trained your mind to correct the flaws you put so much thought into. This process will work to eliminate any character flaws, behavior problems, and unhealthy addictions. Don't underestimate the power of thought; you are stronger than you think. Remember, before you can expect to be successful among others, you must first have the mentality of a boss.

Learn to replace these unwanted traits with better qualities that will help you interact with others. Treat people as you want to be treated even if they don't provide you with the same courtesy. Leadership and composure go hand in hand. Think before you speak-even a fool seems wise when he keeps his mouth shut. *As you become a better person, people will find themselves attracted to you, and with more people to interact with, you will have more opportunities, both personally and professionally to prosper.* The foundation of a good person is his or her character, so it's very important for you to do some serious soul-searching and find your true self. When you are well founded mentally, all of the other aspects of life can be more easily managed.

"Just as a Mason is careful to build upon a sure foundation, you must carefully lay the foundation for your future success in life"

The next stage in your personal growth is becoming the master of your emotions. The majority of the time people end up in some sort of trouble because they allow their emotions to dictate their actions. Emotions have a funny way of clouding our judgment, so in order to make good decisions; we must be in control of them as much as possible. *Understand, letting your emotions cloud your judgment will cause you to be influenced by other people's opinions and thoughts and it will ultimately decrease you level of success in all that you do.*

The key to controlling your emotions is learning to understand their cause. Your emotions are the feelings you get from the interpretation of life's events and your surroundings. The problem is not necessarily with emotions themselves, it is due largely to our misinterpretation of our surroundings. If we would slow down and understand the reality of things much of our stress and negativity would disappear on its own. I learned at a young age that if someone knows how to affect you with your own emotions then you effectively become their puppet. If they can pull certain strings and get a reaction from you, then you are not in control of yourself. The moment I found that out, I vowed not to react to something until I understood it as best as I felt I could. By deciding not to be a puppet, you will be taking your fist step toward being in control of your actions.

All of your emotions need to be, and can be controlled except one. That exception is love. Love is so powerful it cannot be contained, nor would you want it to. I don't pretend to understand love and all of its aspects, but I have been fortunate enough to experience it in my lifetime. At any given time there is only a handful of people who fully grasp this emotion. *Love is a rose stemming from the gardens of heaven. We can all experience its beauty, but its properties are only known among the divine.* When you learn to embrace love it will embrace you back if it is meant to be. That is my experience with the law of love.

"Truth is the child of love and wisdom"

The world can be a cold place if you are not prepared for it. Many of the people you cross paths with are selfish and will take advantage of you if given the chance. Therefore, you must have higher moral standards then those you encounter. Historically, many of the greatest people have used this tactic to find a meaningful and lasting success. When you remove the character flaws that were preventing you from succeeding, you will have room for new and better qualities. *Replace the traits that were causing you trouble with compassion, composure, and prudence. These traits are the building blocks for a successful future.* Learn to apply them to yourself and you will become a person full of confidence and potential.

This is your time to make the necessary changes so you can live a long and fulfilling life. Don't allow your emotions to deceive you on your journey toward a successful future. See things for what they really are and you will go far. With a clear understanding of your surroundings and a high moral standard you will be well on the way to becoming the boss of your environment.

Observe the World...and be wise in its ways.

Chapter Two

Throughout history every man and woman has used observation as their means of gathering information on their surroundings. Mainly, it is used as a basic survival tactic. But, when you learn to observe specific areas in your life and the lives of others you can use the knowledge you gain to prosper financially and personally. This is known among the wise as the "art of observation" When it is applied to business and relationships you will find untold success.

The art of observation has been perfected over the years to bring about positive results for positive people. In the art itself, there is nothing evil or sinister, but just as a weapon can be used for good or bad, so can this. I do not condone people who intend to exploit others weaknesses and those who do this will never find a lasting success or peace. Therefore, you must approach this art with the best of intentions and a high moral standard. The more people who use it for the better, the better off our world will be. Please read this chapter very carefully, it is by far the most important!

"Judge people by their actions"

This first step is learning to identify the patterns in life. It is in the nature of everything in existence to revolve around a set pattern. This is an immutable fact; God designed it that way. Every person, no matter what their age, race, or gender has certain behavioral patterns that they follow throughout their life. These patterns consist of people's actions, and their actions will demonstrate their true character. *When you know somebodys true character, you can appeal to their innermost interest in order to get the results you desire.*

    The things that we refer to as routines are actually set patterns of conduct. A person's routine can provide you with valuable insight into their life. You must casually observe a person's actions to identify the pattern that they follow. Once you have done this you can begin to understand their train of thought and motive behind their actions. It is the small things that reveal the most so pay attention to the details. You do not need to follow somebody to find their personal pattern. Most of the time you can just take note of the places you cross paths with them.

    When identifying patterns, everything is a factor. The places people go, the cars they drive, the people they surround themselves with, the kind of clothes they wear, and the music they listen to all contribute to a person's identity. *The more things you know about people the better you can tailor yourself to appeal to their interest.* The amount of time will vary, but it should not take long to identify a person's routine or pattern. If the process is taking longer than a few months then you are not paying attention, and if you want to get closer to someone, you must pay close attention to details. *Remember, it is the little things that define a person.*

After you acquire the knowledge you need from observation, you can put it to use. Understand that you must be careful, because when you know someone's innermost desires and interests, and you begin to appeal to them, it is easy for that person to become attracted to you. There is a very fine line between seduction and using observation for something positive. It is your good intentions and high moral standards that draws that line, so don't lose your integrity as you begin to discover your new found method for success.

Just as you can apply the art of observation to learn from others actions, you can use it to learn more about yourself as well. When you pay attention to yourself you can identify you own pattern in life. Once you are conscious of the routine you follow, you can eliminate the actions that may be preventing you from attaining success in your life. Usually, the negative actions are going to be related to bad places and unproductive people, but these things can be eliminated by simply removing them from your routine. It is truly that simple. In most cases you will find it fun to tailor your life pattern to bring you more opportunities for success, but when it does become difficult do not get discouraged, just focus on reaching your goals.

"With knowledge comes pure power"

Perfecting the art of observation will help you on your journey to success. When you are constantly observing your surroundings you will be able to see life's obstacles a mile away. This will allow you to be better prepared for the unseen events that occur from time to time. *With such a pure knowledge of your surroundings there is no limit to the level of success you can reach.* Most people go through life ignorant to the patterns that surround them, and had they took the time to learn them, they could have benefitted immensely.

Within the business world you can see where people have tapped into the patterns of life. It is apparent in the services and product they provide that they are appealing to their markets innermost desires and interests. One of the most important aspects of business is marketing. *If a company observes its target market and can identify the patterns of the people it is targeting, it can then begin to tailor its image to attract those people.* In addition to marketing, observation can be used to identify new trends before others begin to notice them; this will give any business an edge over its competition. It is plain to see how valuable the art of observation can be to entrepreneurs and employees alike, and when a company uses the art their customers leave happy and are likely to return.

On the rarest of occasions, you may encounter someone who even after many months of observation seems to not have a set pattern that they live by. It will be wise for you to know that people like that have put a lot of effort into eliminating their patterns. Usually it is to prevent others from gathering valuable information about them. This is the most commonly used by the CIA and other spy agencies as a counter intelligence strategy. To see it used by someone in everyday America is a strong indication that they have something to hide. *The best thing to do when dealing with a pattern-less person is to take notice of the things they avoid, because the lack of some activities will tell you just as much as the ones they perform.* On these occasions the total lack of a pattern becomes the pattern they follow.

> *"He who knows his enemies and himself will never in a hundred battles be at risk." –Sun-Tzu*

Observation is the gathering of information by noting facts or occurrences. When you learn to observe the behavioral patterns of those you interact with, you can then use the knowledge you gain to increase your level of success. Without a pure knowledge of your surroundings, you will be blind, and as a result opportunities will pass you by. As a boss you must be prepared for everything, so observe the world…and be wise in its ways.

The Silent Move is the Wise One

Chapter Three

Every day when you get up and go out into the world you make an impression on people. Your clothes, attitude and demeanor all contribute to your image, but ultimately it is you words that define you. The things you can say make or break you, so when you learn to use the power of words, you can control the impression you leave on others. This will allow you to find success among others no matter what personal or cultural differences you may have.

The power of words can be used to influence other's actions and bring about the results you desire. But before you learn to do all this, you must be aware of the consequences of your words. Most people fail to realize that the things they say can hurt someone beyond repair. When you give someone a black eye it can heal, but if your words are sharp enough, the wounds they inflict can affect a person for life. That is why it is important to have your emotions in check before you interact with others. Just one hurtful remark can destroy a relationship and prevent future opportunities for you to succeed. Therefore, choose your words wisely, because your success depends on it.

The problem with most people is they often say too much. Nobody likes a "know it all" or a "motor mouth" so your first step to becoming the "boss of your word" is to cut out all of the unnecessary talk that occurs throughout the day. Doing this will cause a much desired effect. *It is a simple truth that the rarer something is the more valuable it becomes.* By removing all of the unnecessary speech from your life, your words become rarer, and as result people will begin to value your conversation. In addition to your words becoming rarer, you will also seem more mysterious to others, and this will cause people to be attracted to you. Remember, with more people to interact with, you will find more opportunities to succeed in life.

> "1,000 words left unspoken is better than speaking one word too many." – Anonymous

When your word becomes valuable, so does your opinion. This is why the Bible tells us that even a fool seems wise when he keeps his mouth shut. *If your opinion is valued by others then you can tailor it to help your agenda succeed.* Some may consider this to be manipulation, but if that were true then all interactions would be nothing more than casual deception. What separates you from the con-artists that seek to deceive and take advantage of people is your intentions. You are on a mission to attain positive success, and a positive success benefits everybody.

Once you have made your word valuable to others, you must carefully choose your vocabulary. With fewer words being said you will have less room for error. *If you make the mistake of sounding foolish it will depreciate your opinion and make it near impossible to influence people's actions.*

Therefore, you must observe people to find out what type of vocabulary they respond to the best. Once you discover this, you will have found an open angle to apply leverage.

When communicating with people, it is wise to make them feel superior to you. This will prevent them from feeling threatened or getting suspicious of your intentions. By getting people to speak their mind, you will be able to understand more about their personality and their thought process. Remember, the more knowledgeable you are about those you interact with, the more capable you are of succeeding in life. *Be the supportive friend in order to gather information, and as your friendship grows, so will your status.* Don't be afraid to help others with constructive persuasion as you get closer to them.

When used properly, words can inspire millions of people to succeed. Your goal when working with other people is to make you interest theirs. When you share a common interest in accomplishing a goal, it is more likely to happen. You never want to reveal everything to those that you can influence, just in case they turn sour to your suggestions. Always keep the blueprints to your success to yourself.

As you learn to perfect your mouthpiece, you will notice the changes in people's reactions to your words. *The impression that you artfully crafted to promote success will be causing others to follow your lead, and this will allow you to guide them into their own paths to success.* With success comes responsibility and a boss must never forget that when you can influence other people's actions to bring about a desired result, you become responsible for their well being. That is why you must be conditioned to lead yourself before you should try to lead others. Therefore, respect the power of words and use it wisely.

"Silence is a virtue to live by, respect it and you shall go far"

People Have Bad Attitudes…Not Bad Days

Chapter Four

In life your attitude is everything. It can mean the difference between success or failure. Before you can fully enjoy life you must learn to appreciate it in all of its aspects. By simply slowing down to appreciate life you can change your attitude dramatically.

There are two types of people in this world. Those who see the glass half empty and those who see it a half full. It is up to you to decide which one you are. Your outlook on life can either help or hurt you ability to succeed. A negative outlook is a hindrance on you and those around you, but a positive one is the key to true happiness. Believe it or not, you are in control of your attitude every second of every day. *When you don't allow life's events to dictate what type of day you are going to have you become the "boss" of your attitude.* This is an essential quality that a leader must possess before he or she will succeed.

When I was growing up, I had a friend who always had a negative outlook on life. He was always complaining about things not going his way, and when he got in trouble it was because the "world was out to get him". His attitude was so bad that the other neighborhood kids and I would often avoid his invitations to hang out. I remember thinking how glad I was that I did not have his back luck. But the fact of the matter is that he was creating his own misery by having such a poor attitude. This kid had lots of good things going for him. Instead of seeing the positive things in life he chose to focus on the negative ones, so it comes as no surprise that he has grown up to be negative and unsuccessful. This is a prime example of how a poor attitude can prevent you from experiencing the finer things in life.

It is never too late to make a change. No matter what age you may be, you can always wake up and decide you want more out of life. You need to realize that each day is a new beginning, and yesterday's troubles are in the past. Stop and take a little time to admire all of the miracles that surround us every day. Know that no matter how dark times may seem there is still light to be found. Develop a relationship with God. Be thankful for the good things that you have. Your world is literally what you want it to be so make the choice to live a positive life.

"Success and happiness are the fabric of our dreams"

The three most common factors that influence a person's attitude are health, environment, and relationships. In order for you to truly be the "boss" of your attitude, you must eliminate any and all outside influences. This does not mean that you should neglect these areas of your life; it means you need to have a pure understanding of them. Previously discussed is preventing your emotions form clouding your judgment and learning the see their true causes. The process for eliminating outside influences on your attitude is much the same. *It is done by understanding the role each of these areas play in your life.*

Your quality of health is determined by your lifestyle and how well you take care of yourself mentally and physically. Your health affects how you feel, and most people base their day on how they are feeling. *But when you learn that your day can be full of success and purpose regardless of your health you can minimize the role that it plays in influencing your attitude.* Although, that does not mean that there is not extreme cases where health cannot be minimized to succeed. Ask yourself this, do you think the "Donald Trumps" of our nation allow their health to influence or interfere with their success? Absolutely not. But for many this is easier said than done, so it is wise to eat healthily, exercise, and groom yourself regularly, because a sound body is the foundation of a sound mind.

Your environment is the people and places that surround you. It is easy to see how these things can be an influencing factor to your attitude. If you hang around negative people then it is likely that they could rub off on you. *This is the root of the saying "you are only as good as those you surround yourself with".* For most, this is true because they never learned to block the negative influences of others from affecting their attitude. The key to preventing negative people and places from rubbing off on you is to be aware of the consequences of a negative attitude. Know that negativity is a dream killer; nothing good can come from it. It works like a pitt vipers venom, killing from the inside out. You heard the story of my childhood friend; don't let his mistakes be yours. Rise above the influence of others so you can attain meaningful success in your life. Know your environment and you will prosper.

The people that you have relationships with are different than the people who make up your environment. *Although they still exist inside of your environment, their connection with you is far more intimate. Therefore, their attitudes are most likely to affect yours.* Eliminating the negative influence from those that you have a relationship with is a delicate matter. *If you allow them to affect your attitude then you will never be in control of yourself. But if you pull back too much you will risk being seen as insensitive, and this could cause strain on your relationship.* You must associate with people according to their level of productivity; this will help prevent you from wasting your time and energy on negative people. As a boss you have the ability to benefit from any person or place in your presence, but it is still wise to place yourself around positive people and places. Learn to use others negative attitudes as motivator for your success. When you see someone having a bad day, let it remind you why you are on your own journey to success. Focus on making your dreams come true, because when you are absorbed in a positive mission to reach your goals, the negative things in life will flee from your presence.

Just as negative attitudes have a tendency to influence others, so do positive ones. It is wise to surround yourself with successful people, and when you do, you will find their success can be contagious. When you become the happy, positive, and ambitious boss you are intended to be, you will help others by simple being yourself. *The positive people in this world are like a magnet, everywhere they go, they constantly attract more and more positive people and opportunities to succeed.* So next time you encounter someone with a negative attitude use it as an opportunity to infect them with your positive presence.

When you combine a positive attitude with appreciation for life, you get a winning hand. *Play it wisely and you will prosper.* Know that your best days are ahead of you, and the next time you sit down to enjoy a glass of wine ask yourself…is it half empty or half full?

Fearlessness is the Essence of Freedom

Chapter Five

In life you will be forced to confront your fears. This is a simple truth. Those who struggle to face their fears will struggle to succeed in life. This is a fact. But those who take the bolder approach to life and choose to confront this on their own terms will go on to conquer the world and all of its wonders.

Don't buy into the popular misconception that fear is a natural part of life, rest assured it is not. After all, what feels natural about anxiety and stress? Fear's two closest companions. As you read you will discover how intelligence and common sense can replace the role fear plays in your life. With this new found understanding you will be able to remove the veil of deception that has covered your eyes since birth. *Remember, a boss sees the colors of reality, not the colors of his or her emotions.* Therefore, learn to be fearless, and you will see clearly down the road to success.

Understand, fear is a powerful emotion. Just like a negative attitude, it is comparable to a snake's venom, causing its victim to freeze in misery before death takes hold. It works the same way in your life, causing you to freeze in misery as your dreams slip out of reach. Fear will do more to hinder your success than a thousand "haters" or enemies. Not only does it impair your ability to succeed, it also diminishes your health. It is common knowledge that prolonged states of stress, anxiety, and tension (all symptoms of fear) cause major health problems, all of which may lead to death. This is even more significant if you consider that fact that all emotions have a tendency to be contagious, even if you hide them from others. That is why I put so much emphasis on learning to control and master your emotions in chapter one.

Most people will argue that fear has its purposes, such as allowing us to identify dangers, or assisting us with our overall survival. To some extent this may be true. But if logic is the basis of their beliefs then the same people who make this argument must concede that intelligence and common sense, can and do, accomplish the same things but without the negative baggage of stress, tension, and anxiety. For example, when you encounter something that causes you to experience fear, stop and face it, allow your intelligence to tell you how to deal with the situation instead of letting fear dictate your actions. *When you have a pure understanding of the things that cause you fear you will always be able to overcome them.* You will be surprised how much of a difference this will make in your everyday life.

"When fear is absent, the mind will prosper"

Another technique that will help to eliminate fear is to picture the things that cause you fear as something you love. *This works because it is easier for us as people to understand things we are interested in, and to love someone or something is the very essence of interest.* This is a easy yet very powerful technique to be used by all. You have nothing to lose by trying this out for yourself.

Practice this. Take a moment and ponder your fears. Picture someone or something that you are fond of. There is no stress, anxiety, or tension between you and this person or object. Just a calm opportunity for you to understand something that you previously misjudged. Trust in your ability to overcome anything that stands in your way, and be at peace with this truth. In this calm moment look upon your fears with confidence and understanding. *Remember, when you have a pure knowledge of your surroundings fear cannot exist.*

Congratulations, you may not have noticed it, but you just replaced fear with intelligence. The fact that you chose to confront your fears on your own terms shows how serious you are about succeeding in life. As you continue to apply this technique to yourself it will only get easier to conquer your fears, and eventually this will lead to complete fearlessness. It is said that a man who knows no limits has none, this too can be said in regard to fear. *Learn to see reality, because in life the problem is always smaller than the shadow it projects.* The world truly is a beautiful place.

"Fear is like a foul habit, when disposed of it will not be missed."

Fear was never intended to be part of our emotional make-up. God created us to be intelligent people not fearful ones. The moment you realize that you can begin to make the necessary yet subtle, changes to your thought process to eliminate fear completely. When you reach this state of fearlessness you will be free of all your emotional baggage. This will allow you to see and experience life in a whole new light, a light of liberty. Understand, a boss must be prepared for the unexpected at all times, so as you begin to find success expect the unexpected and you'll never be caught off guard. Use your intelligence to conquer the world and all of its wonders.

"Intelligence. To abuse it is a sin, to neglect it is worse"

Veni, Vidi, Vici

Chapter Six

Everyday millions of people will take a risk and try to succeed in business. They struggle against the odds and hope for the best. Although a few will succeed, most will fail. This is a sad but true fact. What separates the failures from the "lucky few" is not luck at all, often the deciding factor is just pure determination. But in addition to determination there are keys to financial success that when learned and applied will bring you an abundance of wealth. These keys are not commonly known among the average person, and those who are privy to them often lack the ability to apply them properly. Learn to apply these keys and you will rise above you competition in all areas of commerce.

Out of the hundred thousand plus businesses created each year, only a handful will survive to turn a profit. Had others been privy to the simple yet powerful keys contained in this chapter, no doubt they would have found more pleasing results than they received. First and foremost, don't buy the cheap opinion that the reason a business or idea failed is because it was poor timing or bad. There is no such thing as a bad idea, granted some may be better than others, every idea has the potential to succeed. Secondly, any time is the right time for success. I have always believed that timing and conditions are incapable of preventing a person from succeeding. Ideas are like seeds of a tree, provide them with their essentials and they will bear the fruits of their nature. It is up to you to provide the essentials.

Before you can succeed in business you must first have a plan to follow. This will be your blueprint for success. I cannot count how many times I have sat down for fifteen minutes and come up with a plan to help guide myself towards a set goal. It is important you don't rush this process, when you make your own plans take everything into consideration. *Your plan is going to be the recipe to your success in business. Its ingredients are the steps you need to take and the goals you must reach in order to bring about your desired results.* Therefore, it is vital that you have everything in order, because the more complete the recipe is the more likely you will not miss an ingredient. *Put it down on paper to prevent forgetting an important detail, and as you go along make the necessary changes to stay on the course to greatness.*
Never erase any of your previous notes, you will often find that they help remind you of your original goals. Do not be concerned if you find you interest evolving into something greater than you originally intended. It is in our nature to express ourselves in our projects, so trust in your creative powers to assist you with attaining your goals in life.

> "Every person is born with the ability to make money…how much is determined by one's ambition"

Many people suffer from a false perception of the role of money. So many of us spend our lives chasing the "all mighty dollar", and if we get it we often abuse it. Think about how many families and relationships are ruined everyday because people chose to chase dollars instead of spending much needed time at home. In order for you to have a healthy lifestyle you must prioritize your life. *Never confuse greed for ambition.* It is impossible to maintain or create wealth if you neglect other important areas of your life. When you begin to understand these things you can begin to see how wise business men and woman of our time prioritize their lives to succeed. Knowing what is important will be your first step to success.

The first key to financial success is understanding the true purpose of money. *Know this, money is a tool, nothing more and nothing less.* It provides leverage in life and when used properly is will assist you in building your dreams. You have to learn how to make money work for you. Study investment opportunities, know the marketplace, find creative places to get involved in. Know that there is no greater investment than yourself. Don't get caught up in the "money makes the world turn" mentality . Those who live under this false pretense are more likely to fail than a well grounded boss. The fact of the matter is that it is the man that makes the money, not vice-versa. Therefore eliminate any tendencies you have to hoard your money. Invest in your ideas and you will get results.

"You must first let the genie out of the bottle, then he can grant your wishes:

-money

When you look at all of today's most prominent business men and women you will notice they have some things in common. *Although these people are not always the smartest they have managed to accumulate large amounts of wealth by simply following certain timeless keys that promote success in commerce.* When or where is irrelevant to how they learned to use them, but every dollar or possession is a testament to the power these keys hold over the realm of wealth. Apply them to yourself and you will have no limits to the levels of success you can attain.

- Do your own homework. When you know what you're talking about it will show in your actions, others will notice and react to your influence. *Knowledge is power, and in business it's the prudent who will prosper.* In addition, a man who knows his profession cannot be misled by the fools that may cross his path.

- Learn to forecast the trends of humanity. *When you know your target markets innermost desires and interests you can tailor your business to appeal to their needs.* Use the art of observation to get in tune with those you wish to do business with and success will follow.

- Think outside the box. In today's markets you need to stand out from the crowds. Do this by taking the path less people travel and making bold moves. *When there is a method to your madness others will notice and appreciate your ingenuity.*

- Put yourself in a situation where you have to succeed. You will be surprised what you can accomplish when your back is against the wall. When used with morals, the "get rich quick or die trying" mentality can bring you untold riches. *For most of us, being a little desperate is what it takes to push us to the top.*

- Live as though you have accomplished your goals. Remember, a boss is completely sure of him or herself, never committing to a cause that is not positive and full of benefit. Therefore, if failure is not an option you can be sure of your success. Learn to live as though your dreams have come true. *Let your confidence bring you peace of mind...your ambition guarantees your success in life.*

- Don't allow obstacles to slow you down. When you invest your time, sweat, and soul in a project be prepared for the unseen. If you can handle anything that gets between you and your goals you will be impossible to stop. Every move you make will place you closer to the top. *Use every obstacle as an opportunity to show case your dedication, determination, and your perseverance.*

- Be the best. When you are the best at what you do it will show. There is nothing wrong with taking pride in what you do, in fact, you will find that the quality you put out will determine the level of success in business you reach. *Polish your business until it has the luster of gold, others will not be able to resist or deny their attraction.* After all, who can resist the best?

- Never compromise the integrity of your ideas for the sake of pleasing others. You ideas are a representation of you. *If you factor in other peoples thoughts and opinions then not only do your ideas lose momentum, they lose their identity.* Stay true to your vision and in turn it will stay true to your design. Your life is what you want it to be.

- Slow motion is better than no motion. It is important that you keep the wheels on your project turning. As long as there is continuous progress you cannot fail. Get swept up in the momentum on your project and let it carry you to success. Only when you invest in yourself can your dreams begin to materialize.

You will find that if you apply these ten "guide lines" to your business it will bring you an abundance of wealth. But in addition to these laws of commerce the knowledge you gained from the previous chapters will help you succeed in all that you do. Good communication and observation skills will allow you to unlock doors that were once closed to you. Know that the only limitation you are facing is yourself. Be full of solutions, not excuses. You are responsible for your actions, or lack thereof.

"Have a heat seeker mentality, always hit your targets"

In order for your business to reach people you must advertise. Good marketing can mean the difference between pocket change and "Rockefeller money". The only key to successful marketing is creativeness. Throughout history creative people do the best financially. Their ideas have a way of touching people's hearts and minds. When your emotions are in check it will be easier for you to think clearly. Your clear train of thought will allow you to tap into your creative powers. Use your imagination to shape your ideas into something appealing to the public. When your advertisements have a suave or rhythmic message they will attract more business. Intrigue millions of people by allowing your creative genius to lead the way, you won't be disappointed!

"When negotiating, make them an offer they can't refuse"

You can always tell when someone is serious about their business because you won't have to wake them up in the morning, they will be ready on their own. In life, the early bird does get the worm, so stay hungry and you will have motive to get it. It is when your ideas begin to produce profit that you will be inspired to new heights, and as your confidence grows, so will your bank account. The simple application of determination, discipline, and ingenuity will bring about a lasting financial success. Learn to apply this to yourself and it will benefit everyone who crosses your path. *When this happens your "financial conquests" will become "financial adventures" and as your inner entrepreneur awakens you will take pleasure in progress.* Don't be surprised if you find yourself proclaiming, I came, I saw, I conquered (Veni, Vidi, Vici). The world is yours.

Develop a Network to be Reckoned with

Chapter Seven

Behind every powerful man is an even more powerful network of people he has put in place to help him succeed. This network consists of men and women who hold certain jobs or positions that are essential to accomplishing his goals. Each member, whether aware of their involvement or not can be depended upon to perform their duties. Using this power house for drive, the boss reaches new heights of success. *Every string of the web, each piece of the puzzle, is put and held in place by the boss's design. He or she, adjusts every element of the network as needed in order to promote maximum performance.* Everyone will benefit from their involvement in the network. There is nothing evil or manipulative about influencing others to assist you in your climb to the top. Without this network the chances of financial gain and overall success in life would be severely limited. You must learn to find power in others. Develop a network to be reckoned with.

Understand that everyone you encounter in life has the potential to contribute something to your campaign for success. Even a simple minded man can greatly reduce the burden on your shoulders. You can find value in every person you cross paths with, but naturally some will be far better candidates than others. Your task as a boss is to select those who's professions and interests best align with your goals! *Learn to befriend others that are in positions to assist your agenda.* Use the art of observation to get closer to the right people. This will allow you to communicate with people who you normally would not share a common interest with. Let the new friendships be sincere, there is no need to deceive others. *In fact, the more authentic the relationship is the more likely your new-found friends will go out of their way to assist your cause.* By utilizing your ability to observe others innermost desires, interests and over all patterns in life, you will be able to reach across the lines of social circles and interact with many different types of people. As your portfolio of friends and associates becomes more diverse you will discover unusual opportunities to succeed financially and personally.

"A man of many languages is a man with many friends"

So as you begin to vet candidates for your network must remain cautious. Every mistake made will set you back. You cannot allow any person or thing to hinder your success. You time is far too valuable. Don't allow unproductive people to infiltrate your circle. They are the cancer in life that will eat away at your progress. Use the guide lines below to assist you during the vetting process, they must be followed, you success depends on it.

- Those who participate in the network do not need to know they are part of it, in fact, it is better if they don't. *Only you need to know the entire structure of the network, after all...it is yours.* This will give you the advantages of being the only one privy to who is playing what position in the grand scheme of things. *As a result, you are irreplaceable.*

- The truth is contained within the details. Look for people with well managed lives to assist your climb to the top. *Those who are more positive and productive will help to bring order to your network.* Pay attention to their ability to accomplish goals. If they cannot reach their own, they cannot assist you with yours. *Don't waste your time on losers that are content with just getting by in life.* As a boss you deserve the best life has to offer.

- Lead by example, others will follow. As a boss it is up to you to set the pace for success. *If someone is truly on board with your agenda they will not mind following your instructions.* Greatness is recognized by all. Use your confidence to make even the simplest of plans seem grand. Those who admire your boldness and composure will gravitate towards you, these are the people who should be used in your network.

- Continue to refine your network for maximum performance. The moment you begin to slack is the moment your network does too. *You must continually refine your network to ensure the quality of its members.* Never hesitate to eliminate an unproductive element. If there has been a problem or issue with someone before, it will more than likely happen again. *Save yourself the trouble, put people off at the first sign of unproductiveness.* Even if you take a temporary loss.

- There is no limit to how big your network should be. *Everybody has their God given talents, and when you befriend them they become yours by extension. This will contribute to your level of success.* As long as everyone involved contributes to you reaching your goals, your network should never stop growing. After all, who can have too many friends? Let your "black book" grow beyond measure, and you'll have no limits to your level of success in life.

These five guide lines or "keys" are vital to the success of your network. When building your own every person you chose is another brick in the wall. Pick strong people with magnetic personalities. The more careful you are, the better quality of people you will find. Don't rush the process, you will fail if you do. There is nothing more powerful in life than a powerhouse of friends. As the boss of the dynamic, you are responsible for your followers well being. Treat them well, no matter how small of a position they may play in the scheme of things. Let your golden presence be a beacon of hope and inspiration to others. Success is meant to be shared.

In life, people are the ultimate asset. You must utilize every resource at your disposal in order to make your journey to success as swift as possible. Trust in your ability to attain your dreams. Let others do the foot work while you reap the fruits of their labor. In return, help guide them to other opportunities for success, maybe even a partnership in business. Know this, your network is like a spiders web. It may take hard work and time, but it will catch many opportunities for you to feast upon.

Soldiers and Soul Mates

Chapter Eight

The most personal aspect of life that people struggle with is intimate relationships. Most fail to realize the impact these types of relationship have on their ability to succeed. Most of us will go through life unaware of the full benefits that such a relationship contains, and the sad truth is that most will continue to struggle with relationships no matter what they are taught. To go through life without that special someone, without ever touching the truth of love, well…that is not life at all. *Know this, life is about experience, and intimacy is by far the ultimate experience.* You must find someone to confide in, somebody to help fight the battles in life. A true companion will never judge you for your failures, and when you're "down and out" they will pick you up. When pure loyalty is combined with the truth of love, the light of their union will push shadows from their presence. Once you have discovered this in your relationship, and you know how to treat your loved one, together you will be unstoppable.

First, know that it is possible and completely within your grasp to have a satisfying, successful, and truly unbreakable relationship in your life. By following the simple philosophy provided in this chapter you'll be able to turn any unhealthy or destructive relationship into a productive one. Know that every person has the right to pursue happiness, more specifically every person has the God given right to experience love. This means you too. But before you can expect to have a successful relationship you need to understand the dynamics of a healthy companionship. This is actually very easy to understand, so don't be overwhelmed by the weight of these words. The dynamics consist of each person's needs and wants. When you have identified your woman's or man's true needs and desires you can begin to develop a more satisfying and successful relationship. This is essential to a boss's foundation. Learn and apply this philosophy, and let nature take its course. You won't be disappointed.

> *"Love is capable of turning kings into fools, but many fools are made kings through love"*

We all have certain needs and wants that must be satisfied in order for us to have a successful relationship. *When they are not satisfied we lose interest.* Relationships are like gardens in a sense, when you provide it with the water and attention is needs to grow, it will become something beautiful for you to enjoy. But if you lose interest and neglect its needs it will wither into an ugly mess, and you will no longer enjoy spending time with it. Relationships are much the same, in order for it to succeed both people must enjoy spending time together. Without a mutual appreciation between the two there can be no foundation for their relationship to grow upon.

The needs in a relationship are the physical and emotional necessities that must be satisfied. If they are not, there, there will always be some degree of resentment, whether it is admitted or not. The wants are your partner's desires that don't necessarily have to be met. But it is a good idea to consider them, because when your woman's or man's innermost desires are satisfied you can guarantee that you have their undivided attention, and the fact that you have their attention means they are interested in the relationship. *When this mutual interest exists it will relieve you from the concern of having an untruthful partner, and when there is no such concern you can begin to trust.* When you don't have to be concerned about your partner staying faithful it will allow you to focus on other aspects of your relationship. Many couples suffer because they never learned to develop this level of trust, if they had the quality of their relationship would have been much better. Use the art of observation to discover your partners needs and desires, and the interest you create will blossom into a lasting trust. Once you have accomplished this the rest will seem simple.

"I thought I knew what women want, and then I woke up"

Many men fail to realize how much their words and actions (or the lack of) impact their women. *The closer you are to someone the easier it is to hurt them.* That is why it is so important to pay attention to the things you say and do. As men we need to know how to treat our women, and listening is the only way to learn this. Without some degree of understanding you will be limited on how intimate you can be with them. It is sad to think about how many women go through life with a man who never took the time to learn how to treat them right. Most men who do this don't even realize that they are missing such a big piece of the picture. When you mistreat your partner not only are you depriving them of a satisfying and successful relationship, you will be cheating yourself out of one as well. You must learn how to treat your loved one before you can expect to find a lasting success in your relationship.

The key to treating your significant other right is simple…you just have to appreciate them. When you can appreciate your loved one with all of their flaws and bad hair days, there is not much else you need to learn. This is the path to true unconditional love, and when you can do this you will find that all the things you once considered to be flaws are not flaws at all but merely aspects of chaotic perfection.

"Women thought they know what men want, but they were only half right."

For women it is much the same. They get angry faster than men, although they are better at hiding it. This is because they are so emotional. *Their abundance of emotions causes them to be super sensitive to their surroundings, and as a result they often over exaggerate things.* Do not mistake this statement as critical; it is intended to be constructive information. For women emotional problems are the biggest hindrance to their success. Chapter one has a short section on controlling emotions. The information it provides will assist women with relationships as well as other areas of life.

The effect that women have on men is nothing short of spectacular. I have seen the hardest of men turn into cotton from the slightest touch from a woman. It is no mystery that they have influence over men. But when women mistreat their men they are abusing that influence. This is extremely counterproductive to a successful relationship. Just as men should treat their women like a queen, women should treat their men like kings. There must be a mutual appreciation between both partners before their relationship can advance to a higher level of intimacy.

After you have learned to appreciate your partner and you are treating her or him the best you can, you can begin to focus on other important things. But, there may by times that you will have to take a moment and remind yourself how much you really do enjoy, love, and appreciate your partner. This is natural and if you make the mistake of mistreating your partner don't be afraid to apologize. Remember, it is never too late to change for the better. It doesn't matter if you have spent the majority of your life being selfish and inconsiderate. Surprise your partner with a sudden sincere change of heart, and you will find yourself surprised by the results you get in return.

"Communication is simple…just shut your mouth and open your ears"

The most important thing you can do to ensure that your relationship is successful is to work on your communication skills. You must learn to communicate before you can expect to understand or be understood. The most common reason relationships fail is from a lack of communication. If you elevate your level of skills in this area you can eliminate most problems you currently have, and prevent them from reoccurring in the future. When you are an adept communicator not only will you be helping yourself, you will be helping your partner as well. Learn to communicate properly and the success you will experience will grow beyond your personal life.

Communication consists of two parts, talking and listening. It is the listening part that people most of the time neglect. The reason is that when people are having a conversation they are so focused on getting their point across that they forget to listen. When you talk to your partner, no matter how simple the conversation, you have to pay attention to the things she or he has to say. *There is no faking this, because if you don't pay attention and consider your partners words it will reflect in your action, or lack of them.* If you fail to listen it will deprive you of a valuable source of information. The things your partner says are often very revealing if you pay attention. *Each word and the manner in which it was spoken can reveal the emotions and motive behind a conversation, and when you know these things you can connect on a way more intimate level.* A big part of communication is saying the right things. For many couples after the "newness" of the relationship wears off their conversations become dull and lifeless. The solution to this is simple, take the initiative and bring some excitement back into the relationship. This will give you plenty of new things to discuss. By being spontaneous and saying more sweet and sexy things you can re-kindle that spark that attracted you both in the beginning. Do not ever pass up an opportunity to tell your lover how much you are attracted to them.

"The essence of romance is to be utterly spontaneous"

Most people wait for holidays and anniversaries to do something special or exciting for their loved ones. But truth be told, everyday is a good day to be romantic. When there are only a few occasion that you do special things you are limiting your "romantic capability". You need to create an air of anticipation, let the suspense build and never disappoint. When your partner notices how much effort you put into the relationship it will inspire them to do the same. Both you and your loved ones will experience the finer side of companionship in each other.

You can become a "master romancer" by simply putting more effort into making your lover smile. It is the little moments that count in life, so don't be afraid to share more of them. Surprise your partner at work, take them on an unexpected date, and take the time out of your day to show them some affection. Put more fire in your sex life. These are the things that make the difference between average and spectacular when it comes to relationships. When you realize that you are looking forward to the next moment shared with your lover, you can be sure they feel the same. It is important that you don't overdo it. If it is too common then it becomes less special. Try not to get stuck in a routine, because when you can predict the events before they happen then they lose their magic and impact. *Keep your partner guessing about what your next move will be and that feeling of suspense will ensure many sexy and exciting days and nights to come.* There has to be more than just a sexual attraction for true companionship to exist between two people, if you connect mentally, physically and spiritually then you become soul mates. When two people come together they become partners, and the goal in a relationship is to have both the man and woman be their own boss, but unite to be a successful couple. *This is the basis of true chemistry between a man and a woman, and it can only be accomplished through intimate interaction.* When you apply this philosophy to your relationship it will benefit immensely. Every area of your life can prosper when you have a loyal partner to depend upon, so don't hesitate to develop this level of intimacy in your life. Be the "master romancer" and you will never experience a dull moment with your lover. Remember, it is the little things that make a difference in relationships.

Am I my Brother's Keeper?

Chapter Nine

When you begin to experience success in your life it is a wise move to help others succeed too. Not only will you be gaining loyal friend and followers, you will be doing your part to make the world a better place. This may sound cliché, but rest assured it is not. *Every kindness you show to others-no matter how small it may seem, has the potential to change their lives.* There is nothing complex about helping others succeed, and most often it is the insignificant things that will benefit them the most. As a boss it is your responsibility to decide what type of impact you will have on their lives, good or bad, the decision is yours. Learn to recognize those who will benefit most from your assistance, never waste you time on undeserving subjects. The positive publicity and favor you generate will be your reward. Remember, you have the ability to benefit from any situation and everyone has something to contribute to your cause. Discover the power of random acts of kindness, and there will be no limits you your greatness.

This is by no means a new concept. Random acts of kindness have been used for thousands of years by people of every religious and ethnic background to promote success among the masses. Businesses use them to increase profits and promote their public image. Governments, in one form or another, use them for the welfare of the population. But the true worth of random acts of kindness is known best by the individual, and it is the individual who has the most potential to benefit from these acts. When you learn what these "acts" truly are, and you realize the impact they have on people, you will become aware of the endless possibilities you have to affect people's lives for the better. Understand, awareness is a key to success among others. Random or selfless acts of kindness are any benevolent deeds done to help someone without premeditation. It is precisely the element of "randomness" that makes these acts so powerful. The only premeditated factor is the type of person you have decided to bless. When you have a genuine will to help others these acts become an expression of compassion, and compassion is merely an extension of the most powerful force in existence…love.

"What is desired in a man is kindness" Proverbs 19:22

Throughout your life you will be presented with countless opportunities to bestow kindness upon others. It is important that we seize these moments, because we never know if our acts of kindness are part of a "greater" plan to help somebody else succeed. Don't let your busy schedule prevent you from doing good deeds, never rob yourself of a chance to be a better person. Such limits are for losers. One of the qualities of a boss is that he or she radiates compassion, success, and happiness. Just like the sun in the sky, this "radiance" is meant to benefit all who encounter it. So shine your kindness on those who need it the most and in return your own quality of life will grow to new heights.

Don't forget, the smallest things often have the greatest impact.

When I was a child I went with my parents to a gas station, and on the counter top there were these little plastic jet toys for sale. I respectfully asked my parents to buy me one but they chose to decline my request. I begged and even cried, but still they refused. Heart broken and defeated I accepted my fate and left the store. As I stepped outside a nice lady came running up to me with a big smile and a jet toy in hand, instantly my misery was cured. Although my parents did not seem to find much joy in my victory over their "oppression", I could not have been better. You may think this story is about a kid getting spoiled by a complete stranger, but that could not be further from the truth. For me this was a life changing event. It taught me at a young age how good random acts of kindness can make you feel. It taught me how powerful compassion is. That nice lady probably doesn't know it but she changed my life that day, and almost three decades later I still have my jet toy. *She impacted the life of another and in doing so my world became a better place.*

Many of us fail to realize the impact simple acts of kindness can have on others. When you become aware of this it will assist you with your personal growth, and ultimately that will help you interact with others. This will make you more successful. After all, you never know if the jet toy you buy for someone will change their life, but even if it doesn't the smile you get in return is well worth it. Never forget that one kind gesture can change a person's attitude in the blink of an eye. Attitude influences action, and actions always determine results. Do not hesitate to promote happiness when the opportunity presents itself.

Naturally there are two sides to this. Just as you can positively impact the lives of others it is also possible to hinder their personal growth. This only applies to gifts, it is my well founded opinion that it is impossible to harm someone with kind words. When someone goes through life with total disregard for others never considering the needs of their fellow men and women, they will only become more selfish if you give them gifts. Regardless of your intentions, these types of people will not benefit from your acts of kindness. They must go through the struggles of life on their own in order to break their destructive thought process. Still, I find it best to give freely to people you feel are sincerely in need. Such acts of compassion will cause others to become loyal allies. Often you will find that your intuition will help guide you into situations where people are in need. Perhaps this is an effect of the law of attraction, constantly working to make dreams come true. Ultimately you must trust that opportunities to do good present themselves for a reason, and that your acts of kindness will go on to serve a purpose…whatever it may be.

As you go through life bless those you encounter with selfless, random acts of kindness so that they may grow into positive people. Don't be afraid to step outside of your daily routine or comfort zone to help another. *Your attitude influences your actions, and you actions will always determine the results you get in life.* Remember, a true boss radiates success and inspiration, everybody is meant to benefit from his or her "glow". You will find that showing others kindness will bring you much success and it will only strengthen the foundation of your character. No random act of kindness will go unrewarded. Ever!

"He who has pity on the poor leads to the Lord." Proverbs 19:17

Visualize Success in your Future

Chapter Ten

By making some subtle changes to your lifestyle and the way you think you can position yourself to receive God's blessings. I'm not saying that some mythical "cloud God" is going to put a million dollars into your bank account, I'm talking about a universal mechanism that our Creator put in place for our use. The mechanism acts like gravity, constantly attracting things to people according to their thoughts and desires. In the Bible it is referred to as divine favor, in the occult it is the law of attraction, and to others it is known as a type of karma. But no matter what it is called it exists to help you on your journey through this thing called life. For better or worse it is at your disposal.

Everybody has the potential to make their dreams come true, most just do not realize it. No matter what your present circumstances are you can change them for the better through the power of your thoughts. This may sound too good to be true, but rest assured it is not. When you visualize a brighter future you will be attracting opportunities for success. All you must do is take advantage of the opportunities. The first step to making you visualizations come true is believing in them. If I just went about my life wishing and hoping for my dreams to come true I probably would not get the results I would want. You have to believe you will get it. When you're visualizing your future imagine what it feels like to be living in you dream. If you're picturing a new house imagine what it feels like to live in it, how does the new carpet feel under your feet? *See, when you can visualize the details and feel the emotions as if it were real, you can begin to understand that attaining your dreams is not at all impossible.*

"Imagination is not merely a child's toy, it is a vehicle of success"

Don't ever underestimate the power of belief. If believing in a cause can bring about the formation of the greatest nation on earth, then how much can believing in your dreams accomplish? History holds that Jesus cured the blind and performed countless miracles through the faith of His followers. Sometimes all it takes to change your life for the better is a little faith. So learn to believe in the things you visualize, and you will begin to attract them into the realm of reality.

After you learn to feel and believe in your visualizations you can begin to attract them, but first you must know what you truly want to attract. If all you are picturing is a more successful future then that's all you will get. When your vision of your future is distorted and not specific then you will get results in random areas of your life, and not always where it best suits your needs. Therefore, you must be specific with your visualizations in order to get results in the desired area. The mechanism works like a projector, and your focused thoughts are the pictures it reflects in your life. *If you want the best results then you must have a clear perception of what it is you want to attain.* There can be to stray or wandering thoughts as you focus and visualize specific things. Any contending thoughts will distort your mental pictures and cause them to only partially manifest. In some cases a over active mind can completely prevent your visualizations from producing results.

"Faith exists to answer all questions"

The key to having clear mental pictures is to eliminate all distractions that may be causing your mind to wander. This is done by focusing on all the details that make up your mental pictures. When you are busy focusing on how comfortable your new car is it will be next to impossible for you to visualize something else at the same time. Totally absorb yourself in the pictures until it feels like reality. *When you have learned to project clear mental pictures you will get clear results.* I must warn you that this universal mechanism works two ways. Just as your thoughts attract good things they also attract the bad. If you spend your time stressing and expecting bad things to happen then sooner or later they will. This is why it is so important to have a good attitude. Do your best not to visualize negative things, they are extremely counterproductive to you reaching your goals.

It is also possible to visualize and manifest (positive and negative) events and things into other people's lives, but when you do this it will affect you as well. This element of the mechanism is responsible for what people commonly refer to as karma. If you project negative mental pictures into other people's lives you will be bringing it into yours too, because in order for you to do this you had to formulate it in your thoughts, and as a man thinks so shall he be. Therefore, stay positive with your thoughts and you will prosper. Do your best to think fondly of others too, after all, their success is yours. When you have mastered the techniques that allow things you visualize to manifest you can begin to speed up the process. Often the amount of time it takes for your mental pictures to materialize is based on how hard you focus. But there seems to be no time line for events to take place. If it seems like you are not getting results do not get discouraged, when the time is right you will get the results you desire. The last time I visualized something major it took over four years for it to take place. During that time I could notice things happening in order to prepare for the event, and when it finally happened it was even better than I had pictured. So have patience, and you will be rewarded.

The final key for the mechanism is very simple. Take all of the energy that you used to put into negative emotions such as anger, stress, and jealousy, and use it to focus on your dreams. *The amount of energy it takes to sustain a negative emotion can do wonders when it is applied to visualization.* When your entire life is spent on a positive, purposeful mission to better yourself you will no longer have the mental capacity for negative thoughts.

Your life is what you want it to be, and by using the law of attraction it is possible to make all your dreams come true. When you harness your "creative powers" you will be closer to having a life full of success, purpose, and lasting satisfaction. Therefore, pay attention to the power of your thoughts, and next time you visualize something expect to get the results you desire. *Remember, a boss sees possibilities… not limitations.*

"*A man's eyes are quick to see failure, but the "mind's eye" sees only success*"

The Truth, the Light, the Way

Chapter eleven

As you grow into a boss it will be important for you to understand how God impacts you life. But with all the different beliefs and opinions about religion these days it can be difficult to avoid error as you search for the answers to life's hardest questions. When you go through life without a clear concept of God, it limits your level of success to shallow heights, and that causes you to feel trapped between heaven and hell. *In reality there is but one truth seen from many angles, though many of these angles have been misinterpreted and corrupted by man to serve his own purposes.* Understand, a boss is immoveable in this world because he or she stands upon an unshakeable foundation...a foundation of truth. When your entire life is built upon truth there can be no lies, failure, or deception, only happiness, success, and harmony.

This chapter provides valuable insight into the realm of God and how it relates to you. It is not my place to criticize any religion, and I respectfully point out that most faiths do contain some "divine spark"...however little it may be. The words on these pages are not intended to change your beliefs. Rather, they are intended to draw attention to the fact that we as people must appeal to a "higher authority" for guidance and illumination. Simply put, without a relationship with a higher power you will remain lost in a world of failure. Take moment and reflect on how well you know God. You may be surprised by how little you really know. Remember, meaningful success can only come from having a pure knowledge of what your place in this world is, and pure knowledge is a divine gift.

> "I find it ironic that the simplest of men are more knowledgeable of God than the most brilliant scientist."

The problem people have with faith is that we expect to see, or feel something if it is real. When something cannot be physically grasped then it can be debated, and this is the cause of confusion about God. The key to faith is learning that it doesn't have to be based on unfounded beliefs; it can be based on firsthand experience. *When you know the truth for yourself it is impossible to be misled by other opinions.* Consider this: it's not enough for you to just read these pages, you must experience success in your life in order for it to be real. The same concept applies to God. When you have a relationship with your higher power and you experience His blessings in your life, His existence becomes undeniable. But don't be discouraged if you have a lack of faith, you just need to learn where to look and you shall find it.

You can't see gravity but you can see its effects, you can't see air but you know it exists. With God it is even more apparent His effects are everywhere. Most people go through life hoping to experience some kind of grand revelation that brings certainty to their beliefs. We get so caught up in our everyday lives that we fail to recognize that the true miracles are right in front of us. *My friends, the best kept secrets are those hidden in plain sight, and all who are wise enough to observe them are worthy to behold their wonders!* God reveals Himself in the world around us (always present, always perfect). *You will find Him in the smile of every child, in the embrace of every loved one, in the trees and the stars.* He is the miracle of life itself.

"The man who is aware he knows nothing knows a lot." – Anonymous

When you can see God in everything and every moment then a lack of faith will no longer be an issue. Your unfounded belief will be replaced with certainty. That is why it is so important to slow down and appreciate the beauty of creation that surrounds us all. The more you begin to realize how great life is the more in sync you will become with reality. Once you have become such a keen observer you will discover that even the bad things in life serve a purpose. God allows this chaos to take place because it acts like a purifying fire. Those who make it through are refined and free of corruption at heart. *This level of understanding is vital to a bosses' mentality, without it the richer qualities of success will not be enjoyed.* Therefore take some time and look upon the wonders of the world, there is much to discover in life, the beauty of intelligent design is everywhere. Besides, what have you got to lose? You may find just what you've been looking for, perhaps in the least expected places.

Many of us struggle with reaching out to a higher power for guidance but when you know who you're reaching out to you will find it is not so hard after all. *Regardless of what name you use, there is but one God-one truth- who exists in perfect harmony.* Those who deny this display their own ignorance. He is beyond comprehension to all but a few elect around the world, and perhaps the best description of His greatness is His very own words: "I am what I am". God is the very essence of love, compassion, patience and wisdom. In God all things are possible. Although He is the foundation of existence itself He still has more intimate aspects that we can identify. He is the Father, Creator, and Friend who never betrays. He is our guide during the pursuit of happiness.

"Pure knowledge is actual faith"

It is important to remember that your relationship with your higher power is a "two way street". This means that in order for you to maintain a productive relationship with God you must conduct yourself as a God-fearing man or woman. Be courteous, compassionate, and grateful. This is how you give thanks for the blessings you will receive. Stay humble as God pours out His favor in your life, and never fall into the misconception that a man or woman's worth is determined by his or her possessions. All are created equal in the eyes of our Lord. In order for us to truly appreciate our Creator we must appreciate all of His creations.

Perhaps the biggest problem a boss will face during his or her quest for success is avoiding materialism. It is easy to lose sight of important things in life as you begin to experience success, and material things have a way of overshadowing what really matters. Materialism often leads to the final degradation of mankind knows as atheism. Understand: when you spend your life on a quest for material gains you will neglect your spirit. But if you use God as the foundation for your life than the money, cars, and success become the fruits of living righteously. There is nothing wrong with having nice things. In fact, it is your God given right to experience the finer things in life. Therefore, live righteously and you shall prosper.

"The truth of God may never be profaned." – *Karl-von-Eckartshausen*

It is easy to get caught up in the stress of life, but you must never forget to pay attention to the countless miracles that surround us all. Greatness resides in all of God's creations. Observation, revelation and experience are the keys to understanding the kingdom of God and the mysteries contained therein. As you continue to grow into a boss it will become more and more apparent how much God is involved in your life. Learn to trust your higher power and in return you will find the path before your feet illuminated, all obstacles will be revealed as you journey towards a successful future.

"Listen to counsel and receive instruction, that you may be wise in your later days." –Proverbs 19:20

The King's Strategy

Chapter twelve

In life, strategy is everything. As a boss you must learn to develop strategies that can guarantee a desired outcome. *Without the ability to make things happen you will be no different than any other man or woman with a dream.* Results are what separate the real from the fake. The knowledge you possess, your recipe for success, should set you apart from others. You are a unique person, therefore your strategies for getting what you want in life should be unique too. Learn to pay close attention to what works for others, and take note of what works for you. *Remember, a smart man will learn from his mistakes, but a wise man will learn from the mistakes of others.* Develop strategies that will help get you the finer things in life, and keep track of the methods that are most effective…your success depends on it.

Strategy is described as a careful plan or method for achieving an end or goal. It can be applied to anything in life. Many experts expect us to believe that successful strategies are only developed through trial and error. They claim that we must have the "personal experience" to apply our strategies and succeed. They are wrong. *As stated before, wise people learn from others mistakes, but they may also learn from others accomplishments.* If you train yourself to mentally observe other people's means of success, and you can learn from other people's failures, then you can save yourself a lot of work and stress. *When you eliminate the need to personally experience the struggle in order to gain the benefits of the experience, you will simplify the entire process of getting what you want in life.* By simply observing the actions of other successful people, and understanding their methods, you can learn just as much as if you went through the climb yourself.

Know this: anybody can hatch a plan and attempt to accomplish a goal, any fool can have an opinion, but not everyone will succeed. After you learn how to read the benefits of other people's experiences you can focus on applying it to your life. You must compare every situation you wish to change to a more successful model. Find the similarities between what you want to accomplish and what others have accomplished. The differences are the things that separate you from what you want. No matter what you want to attain, the methods to get it can be discovered by following the steps below.

- Find people who have the things you want. Observe their actions so that you may discover the steps they took to acquire the object of your desire. The answers are always available if you just know where to look. Utilize the art of observation to gather the information needed to succeed.

- Compare the difference between them and you. Once you have identified what they did right, and recognize what you need to do in order to mimic those traits, qualities, or techniques, then you can make the necessary changes. Adopt other successful people's strategies to get what you want in life. Don't' be afraid to change for the better.

- Follow through with the methods you adopt to succeed. Since you did not formulate the strategy yourself it may feel foreign when you begin to apply it. Understand, the methods you acquired through observing others has already been proven. If it was not, you would not have noticed and selected it. Trust in the results, if it got them what they wanted it is no far stretch to assume it will do the same for you too.

Observe, compare, apply. This is the key to successful strategies; learn it well and you shall prosper. There is no limit to the things you can strategize to get. Whether it is a car, house, or real estate empire it can be attained with proper strategies. You know what you want out of life, you many notice other people with similar ambition, but those who get results will get the prize. There is nothing hard or complex about utilizing the methods of others to get what you want. When you begin to do this you must add your unique touch to the strategy. You must make it yours. As a boss you possess creative powers and keen observation skills, these skills will give you the ability to turn a good strategy into a better one. Trust in your ability to get results.

Your life is full of chaotic events that prevent you from remembering everything. That is why it is wise to keep a record of successful strategies and lessons learned. This will allow you to refresh your memory from time to time. In addition, you may want to hand down something special to your children or a family member. Pure knowledge and effective strategies for getting what you need and want in life is the ultimate family heirloom. Develop fool-proof recipes for success that can be used time and time again. Reach for the best life has to offer, you deserve it. Don't over burden yourself with work that others can do for you. Learn from the failures and victories of other successful people. Be the boss of your environment… that is your strategy for success.

"True strategy is to build upon the great works of others"

Conclusion

The knowledge you gained from reading *The Boss's Philosophy* has the power to change your life. It is up to you to apply it. Don't waste anymore time. life is far too short. *Know that great things in life are simple and great people know simple truths.* Observe your surroundings, master your emotions, and develop the mentality of a boss. Remember, every trial you go through has the potential to be educational. Have confidence in you ability to succeed. Life is what you want it to be.

I hope that you aim a little higher after reading this. You truly deserve the finer things in life. Never settle for less. Stay strong, stay wise, and never give up. Dreams do come true.

Sincerely P.E. Statler

> *"Your life is like a game of chess. You're constantly making moves. Consider the pawns to be the little battles in life that you are willing to lose in order to position yourself for the big moves… the check mates."*

Acknowledgements

I wish to thank Jacqueline McMurtrie and Fernanda Torres, from the Innocence Project NW Clinic. Words cannot express the gratitude I have for you guys. Thank you for bringing light into a dark place.

Published By:

Rays Of Light Media Services

816 W. Francis Ave

Suite236

Spokane, WA 99205-6512

509-328-2863

509-263-9143

The Boss's Philosophy © copyright 2013

All rights reserved.

www.ingramcontent.com/pod-product-compliance
Lightning Source LLC
Chambersburg PA
CBHW041305110426
42743CB00037B/6